The
GREENING
BOOK

Being a Friend to Planet Earth

by Ellen Sabin

and _____

WATERING CAN® PRESS
www.wateringcanpress.com

WATERING CAN®

Growing Kids with Character

When you care about things and nurture them,
they will grow healthy, strong, and happy, and in turn,
they will make the world a better place.

Written by Ellen Sabin
Illustrated by Kerren Barbas

ISBN-13: 978-0-9759868-6-8
ISBN-10: 0-9759868-6-4
Printed in China

Website address: www.wateringcanpress.com

Dear _____,

Because you are such a nice, responsible, and caring person, I am giving you this **GREENING BOOK**.

As you use it, you will learn ways to make the world a better and healthier place for people, plants, and animals. You will also be making me very proud of you.

You can use this book to do many good things. You will see that you—and your actions—are powerful. You make a BIG difference in the world and you can play an important part in taking care of our planet.

From, _____

Some "thank-yous"

- To Kerren and Sam; illustrator and editor. Their talents and contributions show that a final product is only as good as the sum of its parts.

- To the educators, environmentalists, and parents whose perspectives and input refined my message and words. Special thanks to Susan Sabin, Josh Newman, and Pamela Zuker.

- There were many professionals who contributed their expertise, encouragement, and support. I especially want to thank Gay MacGregor and Tensie Whelan.

A NOTE TO ADULTS

It was a moment when I was hiking and I stopped to appreciate the beauty around me that I understood the reason that I care about being "green." I choose to do things that are green not because I feel that I "should," but because I value my relationship with the earth and the gifts it gives to me. Relationships are two-way streets, and as a sign of my appreciation for Earth's gifts, I do my best to take care of it in return.

The GREENING BOOK is meant to inspire
children to grow their own friendship with the earth.

In turn, they'll come to appreciate the earth's gifts, learn about its needs, and choose to do things to help make the earth healthier...because they WANT to!

Along the way, I hope this activity book will help them learn about the environment, recognize their ability to make a difference in the world, practice responsibility, and enhance their sense of self-worth.

And finally, I hope The GREENING BOOK journey will help inspire children toward a lifetime of habits that protect, care for, and nurture our Planet Earth.

Table of Contents

What is The GREENING BOOK?

Welcome to Your **GREENING BOOK!**

What does it mean to be "green"?

When you act like a friend by doing thoughtful and giving things toward the earth, you are being GREEN.

This book is all about Planet Earth and you and the many ways that you can be green.

As you read this book, you will see that the earth is a good friend to you, and that you can be a good friend back to the earth, too.

Just like a good friend, Planet Earth gives you many special and important things.

The GREENING BOOK invites you to think about ways that the earth gives to you.

- It helps keep you safe.
- It provides you with a home.
- It gives you things that keep you healthy.
- It even gives you great places to see, enjoy, and explore.

Well, friends take care of each other, right?

The GREENING BOOK will help you find ways to be a good friend back to the earth!

- It will teach you about what the earth needs.
- It will help you find ways to take care of the earth and keep it healthy.
- It will give you ideas about how to speak up for the earth so you can protect it even more.

What are you waiting for? Turn the page and get started! ● ● ● ●

How does The GREENING BOOK work?

First
You think about the things you get from the earth that make you healthy and happy.

Next
You learn what the earth needs to be healthy. You will also see that when the earth is healthy, it is a better place for plants, animals, and people to live in.

Then
You think about the things that you want to do to care for the earth.

And You DO THINGS—all sorts of things—to help your friend, Planet Earth. While you are doing those things, you are also helping all the living creatures that depend on the earth as their healthy home.

Then You get to do these things OVER and OVER and OVER again, and make "being green" a daily part of your life.

It's that easy!

REMEMBER: This is YOUR book. Along the way, you can keep a journal, draw pictures, and collect ideas about all of the ways the earth is a good friend to you and all the ways you can be a good friend back to the earth.

Great Things the Earth GIVES to You

People get lots of things from the earth.

The earth gives us things we enjoy.

Have you ever had fun climbing a tree, going on a camping trip, playing at the beach, hiking in the mountains, going fishing, taking a walk with your dog, watching a pretty bird, planting a garden, or doing any other fun things outdoors?

If so, then you've enjoyed some of the amazing gifts that the earth has to offer!

The earth gives us things we need to live and be safe and healthy.

- The earth gives people, animals, and plants their homes. People use its wood to build houses, birds live in its trees, fish live in its oceans and lakes, and plants live in its soil.

- The earth gives us air and water. People and all living things need fresh air and clean water to stay alive and healthy.

- We also need food to live. We get all of our food from the earth.

- We use materials that come from the earth to heat our homes, run cars, cook food, and make many other things that we use every day work.

Many of the gifts that the earth gives to us are called "natural resources." That means that they come from nature and are very important to us.

The earth gives to you and shares with you in SO many ways!

Buried Treasures

Some of the earth's natural resources that are great gifts to us are called "fossil fuels." Fossil fuels were created from material that was buried underground millions of years ago.

Gas, oil, and coal are all fossil fuels.

Each of these fuels is used to create energy. Sometimes this energy is used to make electricity, power cars, heat homes, or run many of the machines and appliances we use every day.

A lot of our electricity gets its energy from fossil fuels. But there are other ways to make electricity, too. Electricity and energy can also be made by using the power of the wind, water, and sun.

Below, make a list of things you like using every day that need electricity to work.

....

....

....

....

....

....

WOW! Now you can say, "Thank you, Earth, for the fossil fuels that you've given me to make all of my things work."

The Food You Eat

Menu

Below, write down your very favorite meal:

....

....

....

....

....

....

....

Ingredients

Now, ask an adult to help you make a list of all the ingredients needed to make this meal:

....

....

....

....

....

....

....

The earth supplies water, air, and nutrients to crops, plants, and animals so that they can grow. Then, those things are turned into food— like the ingredients that make up your favorite meal.

Thank you, Earth!

Fun and Beauty in Nature

Below, write about a time when you had fun outside in nature.

You can describe the place you visited, who you were with,
what you did, the sounds you heard, and what you saw.

....

....

....

....

....

More to do?

There are LOTS of amazing places in nature where you can see
new sights, do fun things, and enjoy your friends and family.

Write about two outdoor places you'd like to visit someday.

Place: _____

What would you like to do there?

_____

_____

_____

_____

Place: _____

What would you like to do there?

_____

_____

_____

_____

Favorite Outdoor Place

You probably have a favorite outdoor place. Close your eyes and imagine it.
Now draw a picture of that place and think about how wonderful it is!

Earth's Animals

People share the earth with more than two million types of animals.

Some animals make wonderful pets. Others are great to admire in the wild or at the zoo. No matter where they are found, the earth's animals bring many people happiness.

What is your favorite animal?

Find a picture of this animal and glue it here.

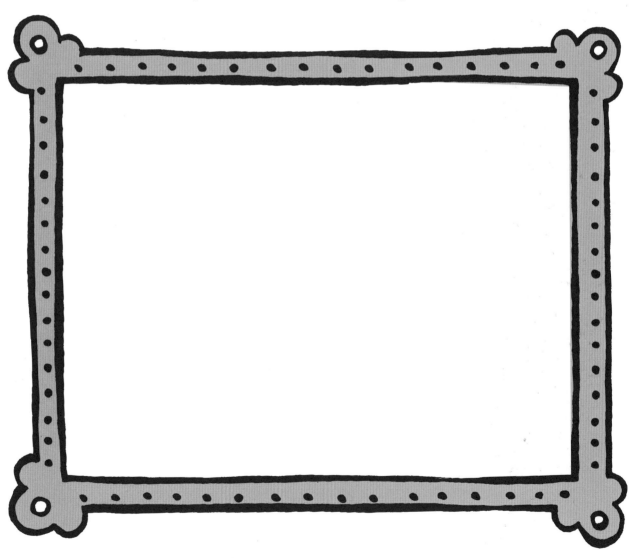

Gifts That Grow on Trees

It's amazing how many important things we get from trees.

Trees produce the oxygen people and animals breathe. They also act like giant filters that keep our air clean.

Lots of food we eat comes from trees— apples, bananas, nuts, spices, syrup, and so much more.

Trees give us ingredients to make paint, cereals, chewing gum, soap, shampoo, tires, and lots of other things we use all the time.

A lot of medicine— even aspirin—comes from parts of trees.

Trees give us wood to build our homes and furniture.

We use trees to make paper books, boxes, tissues, and bags.

Trees give us shade to cool off when we are hot. They also protect us from rain and wind when we are cold.

Trees are pretty to look at and can be fun to climb.

We use timber to build fires.

There's not even enough room on this page to write down all of the gifts that we get from the earth's trees!

What are you THANKFUL for?

Below, you can list some things you are thankful for
that you get and enjoy from nature and the earth.

1. ....

2. ....

3. ....

4. ....

5. ....

6. ....

7. ....

8. ....

9. ....

10. ....

11. ....

12. ....

13. ....

Now, think about other people and even animals. I bet you would like them to have all of those things that you listed above, right?

The best way to ensure that you—and everyone else—can continue to enjoy those gifts is to make sure that the earth is well cared for and kept healthy.

You can start by learning what the earth needs from YOU.

You've just thought about some of the ways that the earth and the environment take care of you and make you happy.

Now it's your turn to think about how you can be a good friend back to the earth.

Part of being a good friend is understanding what your friends need and want.

So, what does the earth need and want from YOU?

The earth is a living thing. Animals, forests, flowers, rivers, oceans, and every living thing needs to be cared for and nurtured in order to grow and be healthy.

It needs people—like YOU—to be GREEN!

Earth's Needs

The earth needs you to:

Understand it.

For you to be caring toward the earth, you need to understand what it needs to be healthy. That means you make an effort to find out how it works, what harms it, and what can make it better.

Take care of it.

Once you know what keeps the earth strong and healthy, you can treat the earth gently. You can do things to protect it from harm and you can also do things to help heal it when it's been damaged.

Speak for it.

When people need something, they can ask for it. They can cry when they are hurt or ask for help when they have a problem. People can even use their voices to join together and make laws that change the things they don't like. But the earth and its plants and animals can't speak. They need people to speak for them. That means people need to use their voices to remind everyone to treat the planet with care.

The earth needs you to BE GREEN!

Take Care of Earth's Precious Treasures

One of the earth's biggest needs is for people to
take care of the treasures that it gives to us.

Why?

- The earth has limited amounts of these treasures. There are only so much land, trees, water, minerals, and fossil fuels on the earth. If people damage them or use them up, some of these treasures will be gone forever.

- Some of these treasures get damaged when people don't take care of them and keep them clean. Sometimes, when places get too dirty, they become unsafe.

- If we hurt or run out of our natural resources, then animals and people would not have things that they need—such as homes, food, energy, and safe air and water.

- Whenever we are given a treasure, it just makes sense to take care of it!

How?

- Conserve. To conserve means to use only what you need and not to waste things or use them up.

- Clean up. The earth needs to be kept clean to stay healthy. People can do lots of things to get rid of litter and decrease pollution.

- Think and care. Once people understand how to help solve the earth's problems, they can show how much they care by doing things that will help the earth.

Being a Friend

You have friends, family, and other people who care
about you and help you when you need it.

Think about all the ways that YOU like to be treated.

I hope that my friends and family will: (circle all that apply)

treat me nicely

be respectful of my things

help me
get better
when I
am sick

notice if I feel
sad or hurt

BE PATIENT

share
with me

have fun
with me

protect
me from
things
that could
hurt me

APPRECIATE ME

give me
attention

be gentle
with me

STAND UP FOR ME

You probably circled all of them!

That means that you hope that people will take the time to understand you,
be kind to you, and care for you!

Well, think of the earth just like a friend. It needs all of these same things from you!

Write down your VERY OWN definition of "BEING GREEN."

_____'s definition of being GREEN:

Now let's see what other people are saying about BEING GREEN.

Ask someone in your family, a friend, or a teacher how THEY
would define these words. Write their definition below.

YOU and Your FRIEND Planet Earth

Understanding Its Needs and Being a Good Friend

How to Be GREEN

Now, you'll get to think more about some of Earth's needs.

You can learn about some of the things that are hurting
the environment and Earth's living creatures.

You can think about the things you can DO to care
for the earth and protect it from harm—
like ways to conserve, ways to clean up,
and other ways to show you care.

You can also think of other actions you can
take to be gentle and nurturing with the earth
so it will be healthy, strong, and happy.

You and Earth's Trash

People use lots of stuff. Where does it all go after we throw it away?

After something goes into a garbage can, it's collected and usually taken to a huge hole in the ground called a landfill. There, garbage and waste is dumped, crushed, and then covered with dirt. Then, more trash gets added, and more, and more. Waste never stops coming so eventually there's no more room left in the landfill. When that happens, the landfill is covered with soil and grass and people find another place to start a new landfill.

Every time we need to start a new landfill, we are using—and hurting—one of Earth's limited resources—its land. People are making so much trash that in some places we are running out of room to bury it.

Sometimes, instead of burying trash, people build incinerators. Incinerators burn the trash so all that is left are ashes. Then the ashes get buried in landfills.

Incinerators help reduce the amount of trash in landfills. However, when incinerators burn trash, they can pollute the air with smoke that is dirty and sometimes harmful.

Soil that surrounds a landfill can also become polluted. Then the crops and plants that depend on healthy soil can get hurt. When soil gets polluted, water under the ground can also become polluted.

Littering is also a problem. When people drop their trash on the ground it makes pretty places on the earth look dirty. But litter is more than just ugly. It is another form of pollution that is unhealthy for plants, animals, and people.

Be a good friend to Planet Earth.

Here are some smart things YOU CAN DO to help
solve some of Earth's trash problems:

REDUCE: If you use less stuff then you'll have fewer things to throw out!

- Use a lunch box. That way you won't have to use and throw out a new bag every day. Each month, you can reduce trash by more than 20 bags!

- If you buy something small, put it in your pocket instead of taking a bag from the store to carry it home. Each time you do this, you're reducing trash.

- When you wash your hands or clean up a spill, you can use a reusable cloth towel instead of a paper towel that gets thrown into the trash after just one use.

REUSE: Some things that you throw away can be used over and over again. If you are creative, you can think of tons of ways to reuse things so that they don't become trash.

- If you give old things away instead of throwing them out, you will be creating less trash. Doing this helps the earth and people, too!

- Lots of paper gets thrown out. You can reduce your paper trash by half if you use both sides of every piece of paper.

- Think of new uses for things before you throw them away! Use an old bottle as a new vase for a flower. Use the newspaper as wrapping paper for a gift.

RECYCLE: Recycling is another way to make trash into something new.

- Paper, newspapers, cans, aluminum foil, glass bottles, plastic containers, car tires, and many other things can be recycled and made into new things.

- Assist in recycling by separating cans, glass, and newspapers and putting them into separate piles at home, at school, or anywhere.

So, before you throw something away, ask yourself if it can be saved, refilled, reused, fixed, given away, or, if not, recycled

Be Green by Giving to Others

Before you throw out something, you can think about if it might have value to someone else. Sometimes you can give away your old things to people who might need them.

Here are some ways to be green, be giving, and do your part to solve the problem of too much trash:

Ask a parent to help you collect all the clothes that you've outgrown. Clean them, fold them, put them in a box, and bring them to a donation center that will give your clothes to people who need them.

Sometimes schools and other community groups have toy drives. That's when people collect old toys and give them to children who may not have many toys. Before you throw away one of your old toys, ask a parent if you can give it to a toy drive so another child can have fun with it, too.

Instead of throwing out old books, you can collect all the books you don't read anymore and donate them to your local library. That way other people can enjoy reading them.

BEST BOOK EVER!

Can you think of other things that you or your family throws out that might be nice to give to other people instead?

Did You Know...

Did you know that many of the things we use every day can be recycled?

In each box below, there are clues about things that can be recycled.
Unscramble the letters in green to find out the answer.

S G L A S = __ __ __ __ __

Where did it come from?
It is made of sand that was dug out of the ground and then melted down using lots of energy.
What can it become when it is recycled?
It can be crushed and melted down to make new containers. It also can be melted to create construction material used for roads.

P A P E S N E R W = __ __ __ __ __ __ __ __ __

Where did it come from?
It came from a tree—maybe even one that took hundreds of years to grow.
What can it become when it is recycled?
It can be made into new paper, egg cartons, even cat litter.

L A S P I C T = __ __ __ __ __ __ __

Where did it come from?
It was made with coal or oil mixed with water and limestone.
What can it become when it is recycled?
It can make lots of things—from toys and flowerpots to rope, benches, and coat linings.

You and Earth's Air and Energy

Air becomes polluted from gases and chemicals that come from cars, factories, electricity, and many other things. Whenever people burn fossil fuels like gas, oil, and coal, we create air pollution. And since we burn lots of fossil fuels every day to create energy for heating, transportation, and electricity, it can add up to a lot of pollution.

Polluted air is bad for people to breathe. It's especially harmful for people who have asthma or other illnesses because it can make them very sick. Polluted air also hurts animals, trees, plants, and even crops that farmers grow for us to eat. Polluted air creates smog and dirt and makes a beautiful blue sky look gloomy gray.

The gases from all the cars, factories, and power plants are also creating another problem. It's called **global warming,** or **climate change**. These gases trap the earth's heat. People are making more and more gases so more heat is getting trapped. This extra heat is bad for the earth because it is making the weather warmer than usual.

If the weather gets too warm in some places, people won't be able to live there anymore. It could also become too hot to grow some of the crops we eat. Too much heat also makes ice in the North Pole melt. When the ice melts, it goes into our oceans and makes them bigger. If the oceans get too big, the water could overflow onto land. The people who live near oceans would have to move their homes. Some plants and animals might even die. As you see, all of these changes could really hurt people, animals, plants, and the planet.

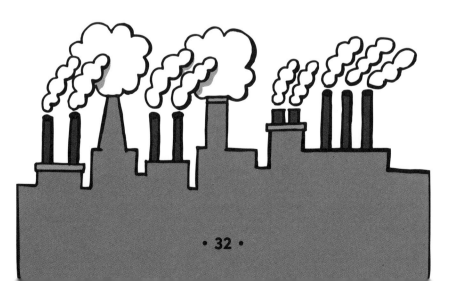

Be a good friend to Planet Earth.

Saving energy helps reduce air pollution.

Whenever you do things to use less electricity,
you are saving energy and helping the earth.

Whenever you leave a room, turn off the lights.

Here's an idea: Make a sign that says "Don't forget!" or "Shut me off!" and put it next to a light switch at home or at school that you or other people forget to turn off. Now everyone can remember!

Turn off the TV, radio, and computer when you are finished using them.
When things are left on, they use energy. You can save lots of wasted energy just by remembering to turn things off when you leave a room or when you are done using them!

Warm air might be sneaking out of your house and wasting energy. To keep the warm air inside where it belongs, you and your family can make sure that your windows are closed tight and that your window shades are pulled down at nighttime. Also, if you find a place in your house where warm air is leaking out, be sure to tell your parents so they can fix it.
Half of the energy used to heat homes is wasted because it finds ways to escape under doors, around windows, through chimneys, and from other places.

Ask your family if you use compact fluorescent lightbulbs at home. These types of lightbulbs use a lot less energy than regular bulbs and they lasts ten times longer.

If every American replaced just one regular lightbulb in their home with a compact fluorescent lightbulb, then we would save enough energy to light more than 3 million homes for a whole year.

It All Adds Up

How many of these things do you have in your house?

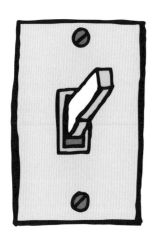  

_____   _____   _____

Now think about how many houses there are in your neighborhood, your city, your country, and the world! That adds up to a lot of lightbulbs, switches, outlets—and energy.

If we conserve energy, then we can make sure that there is enough of it in the future for everyone.

Small choices can add up to make a big difference!

People Power

Some things that help get us from one place to another are powered by gas or electricity—like cars, buses, and trains.

People can make their own power to get around, too. That means you can sometimes use your feet to get you where you need to go. You can also use other methods of transportation that don't need gasoline or electricity.

Using your power to get around is a good way to get exercise, enjoy the outdoors, and help the earth.

Here are some ways that you can get moving by using your own energy and power. Can you find the words hidden in the puzzle below?

```
A S W I M U A K
S K A T E W B E
C B L R M B I I
O O K C A E K A
O A A E A W E S
T F S K S N A K
E A W E R W O U
R U N K W O R E
```

WORDS

- RUN
- WALK
- BIKE
- CANOE
- SKATE
- SCOOTER
- SWIM

You and Earth's Water

We need clean water to live and to be healthy. We need water to drink, but we also use water every day for many other things like showers, washing clothes, cleaning cars, watering lawns, flushing toilets, and much more.

Just like other gifts we get from the earth, there is a limited amount of water for lots of people to share.

The fresh water we drink comes from rivers, lakes, and streams. It also comes from underground—that's called "groundwater."

Water gets polluted when people aren't careful about how we throw things away. When harmful things are buried in the ground incorrectly, the earth acts like a sponge and soaks them in. Once something harmful is soaked into the ground, it can pollute our groundwater. For example, batteries that don't get thrown away the right way can poison water in the ground. Water can also get polluted when people pour harmful things—like paint, oil, and weed killers—on the ground.

Water that is dirty or polluted can harm people and animals that drink it. It can also damage plants and can even kill animals that live in it.

SOME WATER FACTS:

- 70% of people in the world don't have clean water to drink.

- Almost 99% of the world's water is undrinkable because it is salty or frozen in ice caps. That means that just 1% of all the water on earth is healthy for people to drink.

Be a good friend to Planet Earth.

Lots of water just goes down the drain. Saving water can be as easy as turning off a faucet. Here are some ways you can save water.

Add up how many gallons YOU can save in just one day.

Turn off the faucet while you are brushing your teeth	Saves 5 gallons +
Take a shower instead of a bath	Saves 25 gallons +
Take a 5-minute shower instead of a 10-minute shower	Saves 25 gallons +
Tell an adult when you notice a dripping faucet so that it can be fixed.	Saves 20 gallons

=75 GALLONS

75 gallons—that's enough water to fill two bathtubs!

When you add it all up, you can see that you can make a BIG difference in saving water!

Other ideas:

● If you have a garden at home or at school, put out buckets to catch rainfall. You can use that to water your flowers or vegetables instead of using water from the hose.

● If you like to drink cold water, don't let the tap run as you wait for the water to get cold. Instead, fill a pitcher with water and let it cool off in the refrigerator.

● Ask your parents about rechargeable batteries that can be used over and over again. If you use those, you won't have to throw out as many regular batteries. You also reduce the risk that your batteries might end up polluting the water.

⭐ You and Earth's Animals

Animals need the same things from the earth that people need. The earth is their home and, just like you, they deserve to have clean air to breathe, clean water to drink, and safe places to live.

Animals usually get hurt when people harm the places that we share with them. We can all take better care of animals by protecting the forests, oceans, and other places that animals call home.

The number of people who live on the earth is always getting bigger. People are taking over more and more land to build cities. To do this, we cut down forests, fill in swamps, and build in areas that were once homes to animals and plants. When we build cities, animals suddenly have no place to live. As a result, they can become endangered—that means that there are only a small number of those animals left in the world. These endangered animals can even become extinct, like dinosaurs did a long time ago. That means that a whole species of animal dies out and is gone forever.

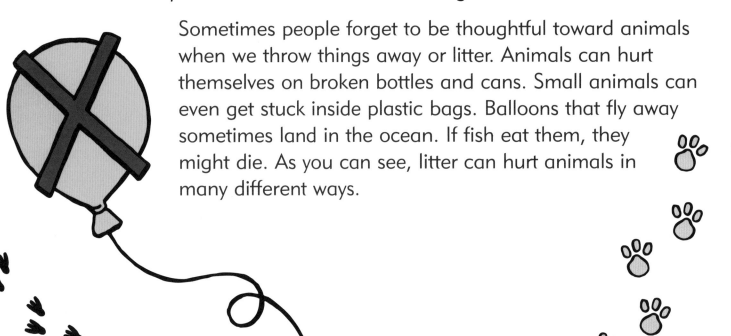

Sometimes people forget to be thoughtful toward animals when we throw things away or litter. Animals can hurt themselves on broken bottles and cans. Small animals can even get stuck inside plastic bags. Balloons that fly away sometimes land in the ocean. If fish eat them, they might die. As you can see, litter can hurt animals in many different ways.

Be a good friend to Planet Earth.

Your actions can help animals.

- If you plant flowers or trees, you'll be giving food and shelter to animals.

- If you pick up litter, you can prevent lots of animals from getting sick or hurt.

- Build a new home for an animal. You can make a birdhouse or a butterfly garden.

- If you have a pet, take good care of it. It needs you to give it water, food, exercise, and attention.

- Learn more about the animals that live all over the world. The more you know about animals and their needs, the more ideas you will have about how you can help protect them. There are great nature programs on TV and information in books and on the Internet about animals. You can also learn more by visiting animals in the wild or at the zoo.

Help Protect the Earth's Animals

When you learn more about animals and what they need to live, you are also learning about how to share the earth.

Thousands of different kinds of animals in the world are endangered.

Do research and learn about an animal that is endangered.
Below, write down what you learned about that animal, including why it is unique, how it is being hurt, and how people can help protect it.

My Favorite GREENING Fable!

There was a boy walking down a deserted beach just before dawn. In the distance, he saw an old man who was picking up stranded starfish and throwing them back into the ocean.

The boy watched in wonder as the old man again and again threw the small starfish from the sand to the water.

He asked, "Old man, why do you spend so much energy doing what seems to be a waste of time?" The old man explained that the stranded starfish would die if left in the morning sun.

"But there must be thousands of beaches and millions of starfish!" exclaimed the boy. "How can you make any difference?"

The old man looked down at the starfish in his hand, and as he threw it to the safety of the ocean, he said,

"I MAKE A DIFFERENCE TO THIS ONE."

(This story was adapted from a poem by Randy Poole titled, "The Difference He Made.")

Your actions make a difference.
YOU can help the earth's animals in so many ways!

You and Earth's Trees

Forests are very important parts of the earth. Trees provide us with food, fuel, shelter, wood, beautiful places to visit, and even life-saving medicines. On top of all of that, forests help absorb the gases that cause global warming. They are also home to millions of plants, animals, and even people.

Forests are being cut down by people who want to use the land for farming or to build homes and stores. They are also cut down by people who want to use the wood to make paper and other things. In fact, every minute an area of forest equal to sixty football fields is cut down. People have already cut down over half of the earth's forests.

Not having trees hurts plants, animals, people, and the world! Luckily, there are ways people can keep using things we get from the forest and keep trees and forests alive and healthy. We just need to be good caretakers. We are good caretakers when we cut down only the trees we really need, are careful about how we take them out of the forest, and plant new trees in place of the ones we cut down. For example, when people cut down only a few trees at a time, then they are making room for young trees to grow big and strong.

People depend on trees today, but we also need them tomorrow and many years from now.

That means we must protect them!

Be a good friend to Planet Earth.

Plant a tree!

If planting one tree is a good idea, planting lots of trees is even better. Talk to your teacher or principal at school and ask if he or she wants to help you organize a tree-planting project for the whole class.

Learn about recycled paper and wood and how people use them to make products so that fewer trees need to be cut down.

Research more about rain forests and the people, animals, and plants that live in them.

If you visit a forest, protect it by walking on trails and not breaking off any tree branches. Keep it clean by making sure to not leave behind any litter.

Here's a project you can do at home: Ask a parent to save all of your family's junk mail for a week. "Junk mail" is the name for all the letters, catalogs, and magazines that you didn't ask for and that you usually don't want. Look through all the junk mail for the name of the person or company that sent it to you. Then you can call them or write them an email or letter telling them to please stop sending you unwanted mail. Let them know that you would prefer to save the trees!

More Questions?

You've just learned a lot about the earth and some of its problems and needs.

An important part of being a friend is learning all you can about your friends. Here's your chance to learn even more about your friend Planet Earth.

Fill in the answers to these questions when you have learned them.

How are the sun, wind, and water used to create energy?

_____

_____

_____

_____

How does clean water get to the faucet in my house?

_____

_____

_____

_____

What is a "carbon footprint?"

_____

_____

_____

_____

_____

If you have more questions, write them down and then try to find the answers.

Want to Do Even More?

Join an environmental club

Plant a garden

Organize a litter clean-up day

Teach someone about recycling

Refill your empty water bottles

Reuse plastic bags

Put leaves in bags for recycling

Sponsor an endangered animal

Return bottles to stores or recycling centers

Thank someone if you see them doing something nice for the earth

Trade your used books with friends

Use a fan instead of using air conditioning to cool off

Throw an Earth Day party

SPEAK UP
for the Earth

SAVE THE PLANET

You can **SPEAK UP** for the earth by learning about what the earth needs and then teaching other people and taking action.

You can even get your friends together to help. After all, if one person can do many good things to speak up for the earth, a group of people can do even more!

Teach Others

You and your friends can do research and learn even more about an environmental issue. Then each of you can write a report about the things you learned and present it to your class.

Raise Money

A wonderful way to show that you care about the earth is to help raise money for organizations that try to solve some of the problems facing the earth. You and your friends can make drawings, paintings, and crafts. Then you can set up a stand to sell the art. Donate the money you earned to an organization that helps the environment.

Your Voice Matters...Speak UP!

Trees, flowers, animals, soil, air, and water can't talk. But YOU can!

Now that you know more about what the earth needs and ways people can protect and care for it, you can speak up for it.

You don't need to litter. I'll throw that away for you.

No, thank you. I don't need a bag. We brought our own cloth bag to use.

Does my school turn off the lights, heat, and air conditioning when no one's there?

There are no recycling bins here. Can I help start a recycling program?

Let's do something outside and enjoy nature today!

Write a Letter

Another way to speak up is to write down how you feel.

The president, senators, governors, and other leaders need to know how people think and feel about environmental issues. Your opinions can help them make laws that will keep the earth safe.

Your ideas are important, so write letters. You can start with this one.

Dear _____,

_____

_____

_____

_____

_____

_____

_____

_____

From, _____

Learn about Some Environmental Heroes

There are many people who have made a difference in protecting the animals we live with, the air we breathe, the food we eat, and the places we enjoy.

Ask your parents or do research in the library or on the Internet about the people listed below. Then tell your friends about your favorite environmental hero from history.

Gaylord Nelson
What did he do?

Jacques Cousteau
What did he do?

Mardy Murie
What did she do?

John Muir
What did he do?

Here are some more environmental heroes from history:

Rachel Carson, Dian Fossey, Aldo Leopold, and Teddy Roosevelt.

There are also lots of people living today who are environmental heroes!
Can you think of some?

You are a HERO, too!

You already know that what you say and what you do can make a difference in the world. Ordinary people—like the environmental heroes you just learned about—often do extraordinary things!

Write about something you dream about doing that would make you an environmental hero.

Show Your Earth Messages in Your Art

Sometimes people forget to think about the earth.
You can remind them through your art!

Make a T-shirt and wear it proudly.

I RECYCLE!

CONSERVATION IS COOL!

I ♥ TREES!

What else can you write on your T-shirts?

You can also share your message through art by making posters, writing poems, or creating songs.

Start a Trend

Sometimes all it takes to get a group of people to join in a good idea is for ONE person to take the lead and start a project.

Here's what leaders do and one idea for a project:

 ## Leaders learn the facts.

Did you know that cell phones and computers can be recycled, but that most people throw them away? Even cartridges that supply ink for computer printers can be recycled. When these cartridges are not recycled, they can pollute water and add millions of pounds of trash to landfills. Sadly, less than 10% of ink cartridges get recycled.

 ## Leaders teach others.

You can make posters to share facts about recycling. Put these posters up in your school and community. Then your classmates and neighbors will see why it's such a good idea to recycle cell phones, computers, and ink cartridges.

 ## Leaders suggest solutions.

On your posters, you can ask people to bring in their used cell phones, computers, and ink cartridges. Put boxes underneath the signs so people can have a place to leave their things. When the boxes are filled, you and your friends—along with a parent or teacher—can bring these things to a place to be recycled.

 ## Leaders stick with it.

You can repeat this recycling project over and over again. Every time you do it you will be helping the earth. You can even ask other people to use your idea and put signs and bins in other schools and communities. Watch your idea spread.

You can probably think of many other projects that can make the earth healthier and safer.

Get Your Family and Friends Involved

When you talk to other people about being good to the earth, you can get them excited to get involved. Start with your family. Share your ideas about being green with them and ask them about their ideas. Then, you and your family can write a "family promise." This is a list of ways that you all want to help the environment.

Our Family Promise

We all promise to be green by:

- ....
- ....
- ....
- ....
- ....

Our family's actions will help the earth stay healthier and safer.

Family signatures:

....

....

Now that you know how to get other people excited and involved in helping the earth, how about getting your classmates together and writing a "class promise." Friends in your neighborhood can write a "neighborhood promise."

Keep an Eye on Your Wishes

Sometimes it helps to make your wishes come true by writing them down and keeping an eye on them!

Here's an art project idea: Get together with your friends or family and create a "Wishes for the Earth" wall. Here's how:

3. Hang your paper Earth Wishes on the wall at your home or school.

1. Take several big pieces of paper, cut them into circles, and draw on them so they look like the earth.

2. On each circle, write down the things that you wish people would do to be kind to the earth and protect it.

Then you can see everyone's Earth Wishes on the wall and be one step closer to making them come true!

YOU Are So Green!

Draw a Picture

Draw a picture of YOU doing something that is helpful and giving to the earth.

....

WRITE YOUR NAME HERE

Makes the World a Better Place!

Every time you do something giving and kind for the planet, write about it here. You can write about when you help animals, conserve the earth's resources, recycle, clean up, donate used items, and anything else you do for the earth and its living creatures.

Date:

What did you do?

Date:

What did you do?

Date:

What did you do?

Date: ....
What did you do?

....
....
....
....

Date: ....
What did you do?

....
....
....
....

Date: ....
What did you do?

....
....
....
....

Date: ....
What did you do?

....
....
....
....

Don't you feel great about yourself when you help the earth?

OTHER STUFF

YAY YOU!

Congratulations!

You've learned a lot about the earth and its treasures.
This GREENING BOOK certificate shows that you take time
to appreciate and understand the earth and that you do many
things that help care for, protect, and nurture the earth.

THE GREENING BOOK

This certificate is awarded to

....

WRITE YOUR NAME HERE

for being concerned, caring,
and good to Planet Earth.

....

DATE

Now it's your job to spread the word!

Now that you know how great it feels to help make the earth healthy, get out
there and tell your friends and family how important it is. The more people who
learn about ways to be good to the earth, the better our world will be.

♥ Other Ways to Be Green ♥

People can make lots of other choices that help the earth.

Below, you can read about some things that people, groups, and even businesses are doing to help the planet.

SHOPPING CHOICES

Some people are "green" consumers. That means that they choose to buy certain kinds of cars, food, clothes, toys, and other things based on the impact these goods have on the earth.

POWER CHOICES

More and more people are choosing to use alternative, "renewable" sources of energy to power their homes or things. That means that they use types of energy that will never run out. Instead of using gas or oil, they use solar energy (energy from the sun) or energy from the wind or water.

BUSINESS CHOICES

Some companies are choosing to be more "green." They try to treat the earth more gently when they run their business or make products. If you see a truck or car that says "SmartWay® Transport" you'll know that that company is trying to be earth-friendly by using  fewer fossil fuels and reducing air pollution. Other companies make products that use less energy. For example, many appliances and household items— like refrigerators, computers, dishwashers, and TVs— have earned the "ENERGY STAR®" label. Products with that label use a lot less energy and help fight global warming.

TRANSPORTATION CHOICES

Some people like to carpool or take buses or trains instead of driving alone. By traveling in groups, people use fewer cars. Fewer cars on the road means less gas is used and less pollution is created.

Join Watering Can® Press in growing kids with character.

www.wateringcanpress.com

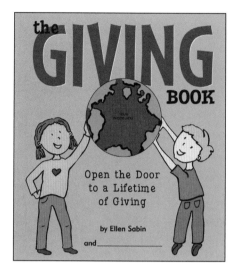

the **GIVING** BOOK

Open the Door to a Lifetime of Giving

by Ellen Sabin

and_____

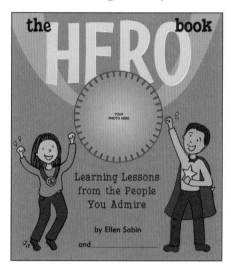

the **HERO** book

YOUR PHOTO HERE

Learning Lessons from the People You Admire

by Ellen Sabin

and_____

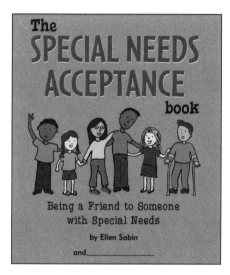

The **SPECIAL NEEDS ACCEPTANCE** book

Being a Friend to Someone with Special Needs

by Ellen Sabin

and_____

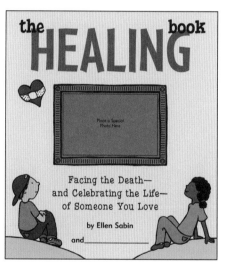

the **HEALING** book

Place a Special Photo Here

Facing the Death— and Celebrating the Life— of Someone You Love

by Ellen Sabin

and_____

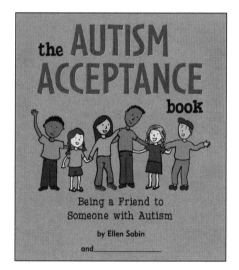

the **AUTISM ACCEPTANCE** book

Being a Friend to Someone with Autism

by Ellen Sabin

and_____

Customized Books for your company or organization

- See other Watering Can® series books.
- Order books for yourself or to donate to an organization of your choice.
- Take advantage of bulk discounts for schools and organizations.
- Learn about customizing our books for corporate and community outreach.
- View the FREE Teacher's Guides and Parent's Guides available on our site.

We hope that you've learned a lot about how the earth is a good friend to you and how you can be a good friend back to the earth.

This book uses paper originating from well-managed, controlled forests and includes recycled wood or fiber.

Certified by the Forest Stewardship Council.

The plastic used for binding this book was also made from recycled material.